32 *Steps:*

Our Evolving Humanity And The Inevitability Of Lasting Peace

Kathryn Colleen, PhD RMT

Trend Factor Press

Trend Factor Press, a division of Sparticle Concepts LLC
1530 P B Lane #M4819, Wichita Falls, TX 76302-2612
KathrynColleen.com

ISBN 978-1-7356943-3-7 (paperback, English)
ISBN 978-1-7356943-4-4 (ebook, English)
ISBN 978-1-7356943-5-1 (audiobook, English)

To contact the author, or to find more information, please visit
KathrynColleen.com. Your thoughts and questions are
welcomed.

Cover art by Kathryn Colleen, PhD RMT

TABLE OF CONTENTS

–

The Evolving Individual

–

Your Destination Is Unique - The Road To Get There Is NOT
10

What You Get When You Put It All Together - The Cycle of Human Development
17

Stage One: Everything Is Me
21

Stage Two: I Am Everything Except Experiences And Reflexes
23

Stage Three: I Am My Needs
26

Stage Four: Others Have Needs Too (I Am My Needs And Others Are Their Needs)
29

Stage Five: I Am My Value Set / Ideology / Religion / Beliefs
32

Stage Six: To Each Their Own (I Am My Ideology And Others Are Their's)
35

Stage Seven: Questioning Everything
38

Stage Eight: I Am A Child Of The Universe/Divine
42

Stage Nine: I Am A Consciousness Trapped In This Body
44

Stage Ten: I Am The ONE Consciousness
46

Stage Eleven: I Am The One Consciousness And The Physical Manifestation Simultaneously And There Is No Difference
48

The Key To Your Journey - CONNECTION
51

—

Our Evolving Societies

—

Does Society As A Whole, Develop Along The Cycle Just Like An Individual? YES!
54
The Stage One Society - Open
60

The Stage Two Society - Experiences
62
The Stage Three Society - Needs
64
The Stage Four Society - The Needs Of Others
67
The Stage Five Society - Ideology
70
The Stage Six Society - Live And Let Live
73
The Stage Seven Society - Questioning Everything
76
The Stage Eight Society - Purpose
79
The Stage Nine Through Eleven Society - Consciousness,
Oneness And Transcendence
81

–

Our Evolving Humanity Through Time

–

Human History Through The Stages
86
Stepping "Backwards"
89

Exponential Progress
94

–

Where We Will Go From Here

–

Global Awakening
98
Future Conflict / Pandemic
101
The Age Of Peace
103
The Age Of Consciousness
107

–

Getting There

–

Is It Possible To Move Entire Societies Into Another
Stage? Yes. But Be Ethical About It.
112
Global Peace In Our Lifetime - Covering Humanity In 32
Steps
118

–

Support For Your Journey

–

Kathryn Colleen, PhD RMT

LastingPeace.org
126
Starting To Mentor Others
127
Questions, Answers And Additional Resources
131
About The Author
132

32 Steps

———

The Evolving Individual

———

Your Destination Is Unique - The Road To Get There Is NOT

Society and humanity at large are just a collection of individuals. When we think about how a society is changing, what we are really observing is how the individuals are evolving, collectively. Therefore, the first thing we need to understand is how we evolve as individuals. If you can understand your own evolution, you can understand humanity's evolution, because they are the same.

I went through the same journey of personal discovery that everyone goes through at some point. Reflecting on my own journey, I wondered if what I went through was unique in some way. I found that, although my purpose here in this life and my personality are unique, the journey of discovery was not at all unique. Not only that, I was not even the first person to try and pick it apart.

I found that many before me had documented stages of human development and suggested a series of stages that we all go through. Kegan documented social development stages. Fowler documented religious development stages.

Then I did my own digging around. Clearly, people like the Dalai Lama, Mother Theresa, Gandhi, Mandela, and other significant figures had gotten much farther. What were their additional stages? In the end, I found that each of these sets of stages had significant overlap and linked up nicely to form a single coherent cyclical path of development. Let's look at the pieces.

Although your hopes and dreams and the life you ultimately want to craft for yourself are completely unique to you, what you are experiencing right now in your desire for self-development is not unique. You are in great company. Each of us here in the human experience develops along the same path from birth.

No matter what country you were born in, what political affiliation you currently ascribe to, what religion you grew up with, or what language you speak, you have been evolving along a set of eleven specific stages since birth. At every moment of every day, you are experiencing one of these eleven stages, whether you realize it or not.

Let's look at some of the early research...

Let's start with Maslow's Hierarchy of Needs. It maps into stages of development as seen here. Dr. Abraham Maslow noticed that we have changing needs over the course of our lives. At first, we are primarily concerned with the basics like food, shelter and clothing. Once those needs are fulfilled, we begin to seek other things like safety and health, love, belonging, esteem, and self-actualization.

Maslow's
Hierarchy
Of Needs

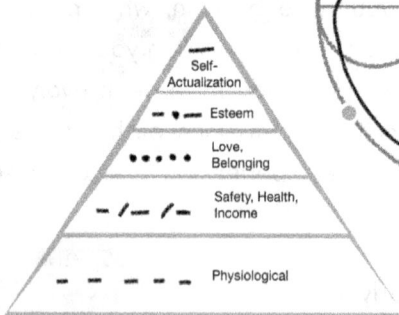

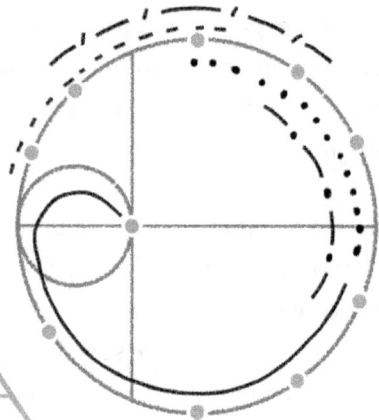

Self-Actualization

Esteem

Love, Belonging

Safety, Health, Income

Physiological

The chakra system is another widely used concept that formed (among other things) an early exploration into how we evolve over the course of our lives. Chakras are energy centers throughout the body thought to be linked to specific concepts like safety, compassion, and expression. The chakras also map to a development process as seen here. You can see common themes here with Maslow's hierarchy of needs.

The Chakra System

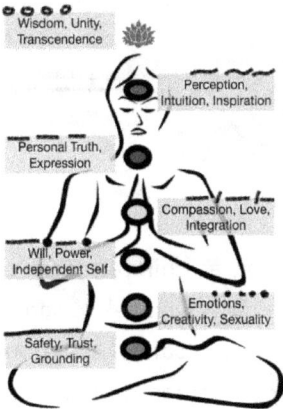

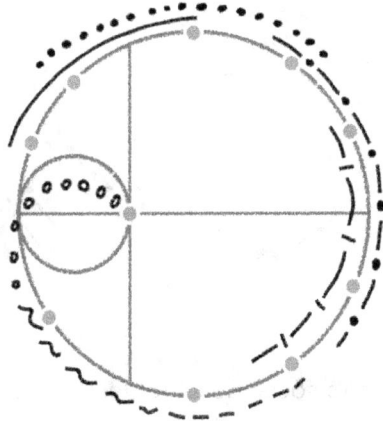

Wisdom, Unity, Transcendence

Perception, Intuition, Inspiration

Personal Truth, Expression

Compassion, Love, Integration

Will, Power, Independent Self

Emotions, Creativity, Sexuality

Safety, Trust, Grounding

Many other psychologists and thought leaders had similar ideas, each detailing portions of a larger cycle of development. Seen here are just a few of the more prominent names and where their work fits in.

The Shoulders of Giants - Stages Of Human Development

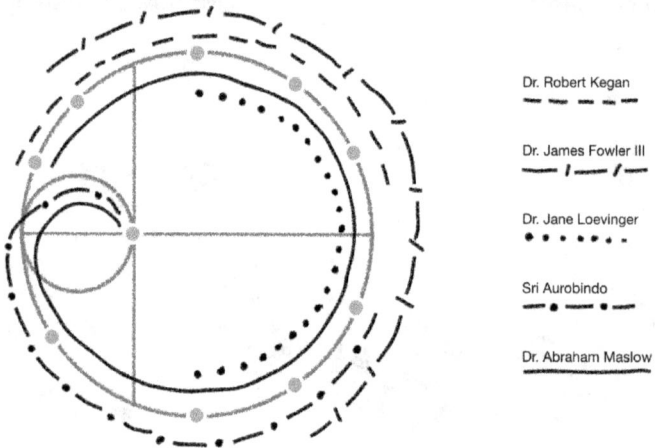

Dr. Robert Kegan

Dr. James Fowler III

Dr. Jane Loevinger

Sri Aurobindo

Dr. Abraham Maslow

Kegan's social development comes first, as children learn to navigate the social world. At the same time, we seek to satisfy our needs for food, shelter, clothing and safety. Religious development, as documented by Fowler comes soon after as we make sense of the world. Soon enough, we find ourselves driven by ideologies, and then by longing for deeper meaning, as documented by Dr. Jane Loevinger and Sri Aurobindo

We see specific themes within their work that suggest four distinct quarters of this cycle.

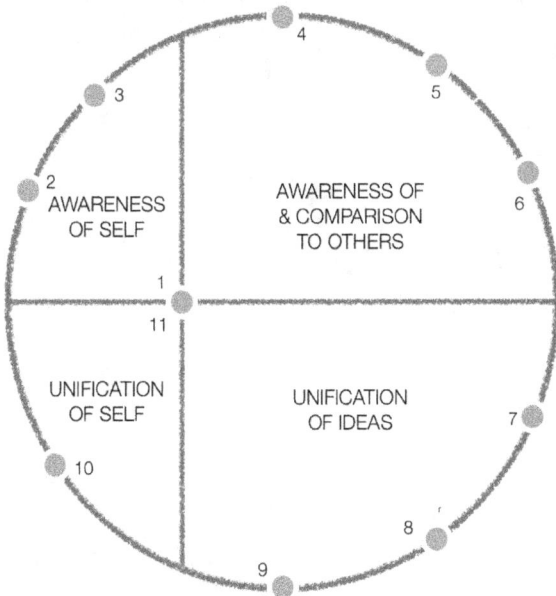

We begin by becoming aware of ourselves, then we become aware of others and their ideas and we compare ourselves to them. We then transition to unifying those ideas, and lastly to unifying ourselves.

If you can become aware of even simply what quadrant you are experiencing today, you can help yourself move along this development cycle more effectively and efficiently.

What You Get When You Put It All Together - The Cycle of Human Development

There are eleven stages of development that you CAN experience. (That does not guarantee that you will.)

Almost everyone wakes up at some point in their lives (usually between stages three and six). Some call it a midlife crisis. These days there is also a quarter-life crisis. Some people wake up much later and some not at all. Some wake up and decide to not take the journey and essentially go back to sleep.

Earlier stages are not lesser; in fact, they are essential and must be completed, or you will keep being pulled back into them again and again. The large majority of people in the western world do not make it past stages five or six and spend most of their days there, happily enough.

These eleven stages are not a staircase or a straight line of milestones to be achieved. They are not a race for achievement. They are a circle - a cycle of human development that we traverse over and over, trying to pick up the pieces and complete stages as we revisit them again over the course of our lives. Even as you spend more time in later stages, you will periodically be pulled back to earlier stages by major life events (injury, family issues, election cycles, etc).

You cannot avoid coming around the cycle again and again. But you can spend a lot less time in these earlier stages where life is hard and negative emotions dominate; and you can spend a lot more time in later stages where life is easy, joyous, fulfilling and peaceful.

Stage one and stage eleven are essentially the same (with some added richness). The irony that we enter this world with the right idea and then must work our way back to it, is rather funny. The universe has a sense of humor.

Ask yourself: which stage do you find yourself in most of the time? As you go through your day, try to step back from yourself and see where you are on this cycle. Some days, you might traverse the entire cycle in one day. Other days might find you specifically in one stage or another.

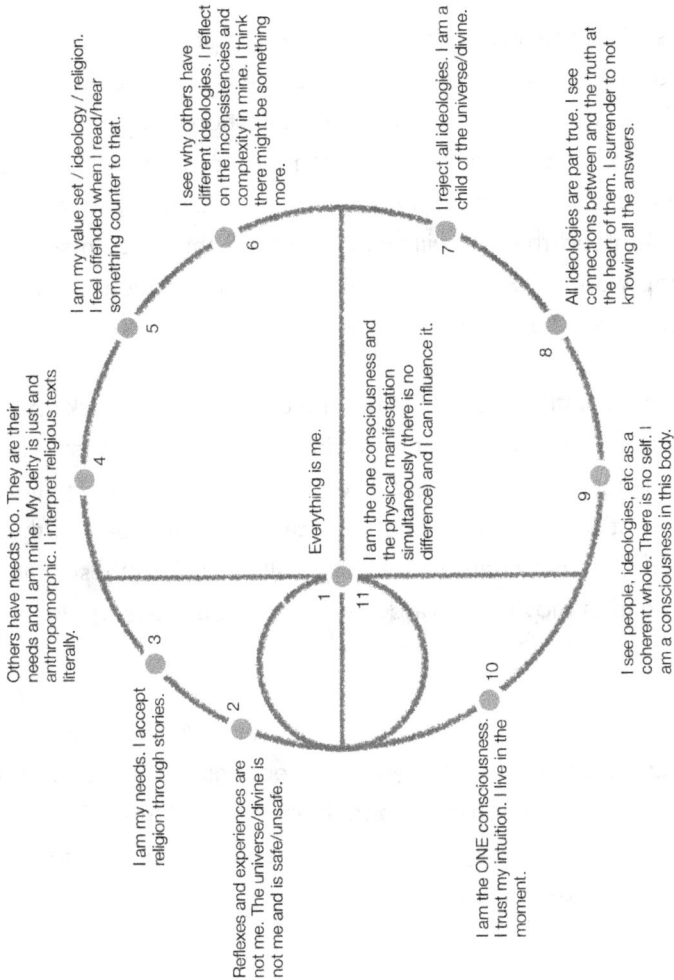

I see why others have different ideologies. I reflect on the inconsistencies and complexity in mine. I think there might be something more.

6

I am my value set / ideology / religion. I feel offended when I read/hear something counter to that.

5

I reject all ideologies. I am a child of the universe/divine.

7

All ideologies are part true. I see connections between and the truth at the heart of them. I surrender to not knowing all the answers.

8

Others have needs too. They are their needs and I am mine. My deity is just and anthropomorphic. I interpret religious texts literally.

4

Everything is me.

I am the one consciousness and the physical manifestation simultaneously (there is no difference) and I can influence it.

9

I see people, ideologies, etc as a coherent whole. There is no self. I am a consciousness in this body.

I am my needs. I accept religion through stories.

3

1

11

Reflexes and experiences are not me. The universe/divine is not me and is safe/unsafe.

2

10

I am the ONE consciousness. I trust my intuition. I live in the moment.

Based on the stage where you tend to spend the most time, you have some work to do. Each stage has a set of important tasks that must be addressed and questions that you can use to help complete that stage and move yourself to the next. If you leave something undone at one stage, you can be guaranteed that life will bring you back there again soon to keep working. So be proactive yet patient about it and try to complete each stage's tasks as you go.

It is most efficient to start from the beginning and pick up any pieces you have left undone in earlier stages. Most adults wake up between stages five and six, but have significant tasks still to do from stages one through four. Leaving these tasks undone means you will be pulled back to these stages instead of moving forward. It will delay your development. So start at Stage One.

Below is a short description of each stage. As you read about each stage here, see if you can recognize it in yourself, in your town, your nation, and humanity at large. For more detail on each stage's tasks, and recommended resources, see the book *Purna Asatti*.

Stage One: Everything Is Me

Characteristics

- A newborn infant (open).

- Other people are not separate from you.

- Your experiences define you.

Challenges

When you are in this stage, you can tend to obsess over the stories of your past and present; times when you were wronged. You can tend to focus on describing your current situation (for the story you will tell about it later), rather than making conscious choices about what you want your situation to be and taking action to change it. You can also feel overwhelmed at the journey ahead of you.

Tasks

Grounding Yourself...

- Declutter your schedule, your attention and your spaces to focus on this process.

- Choose a form of meditation or prayer. Set aside some time each day and hold it sacred.

Learning To Trust...

- Understand the emotional roots of your choices.

- Learn to trust yourself.

- Learn to trust the Universe/River/Divine.

Stage Two: I Am Everything Except Experiences And Reflexes

Characteristics

- A young infant or child (open, learning, new)

- Impulsive

- A sense of the universe or divine as generally safe or unsafe

Challenges

In this stage, you can tend to neglect your needs by simply not knowing what they are. Traumatic events and major life experiences can pull you back to this stage as you try to process what has occurred and detach from it. That takes real effort and your needs can sometimes be neglected because they may have changed.

Tasks

Connect to experiences...

- Manifest the experiences you want, understanding that they teach you but are not you.

- Don't waste time on the past, except to see how far you have come and to be thankful for that.

Connect to your needs...

- Evolve your list of needs as you learn about yourself and grow. Keep this list of needs somewhere close so you can refer to it.

Connect to your body...

- Ensure that you are getting enough sleep.

- Make time for regenerative activities such as hot baths, time alone, massage, exercise, meditation or prayer, etc.

- Start moving. Choose a form of movement and engage with it most days.

Stage Three: I Am My Needs

Characteristics

- Focused on what you perceive as your needs: food, sleep, attention, sex, money, etc.

- Other people are not individuals with needs but reflexes you can bring to bear to fulfill your own needs.

- Religion is learned through stories, experiences, images and people. Sense is made of religion based on how it can help fulfill your needs; what it can do for you.

Challenges

This is a very self-focused stage where you need to defend and fulfill your needs. However, it can be a stage where others are neglected as the collateral damage of your self-focused efforts. This can lead to alienating friends and family. It can turn you into a self-centered jerk that no one wants to be around. You must find a way to balance the fulfillment of your needs without using others and without disregarding the fact that they have needs too. This stage is very common in children and some young adults. Crisis, injury, surgery, and other medical issues will easily draw you back to this stage at any age. Because it is so self-focused, this stage is a great time to start examining your baggage from past relationships and childhood as well as an ideal stage to get out of debt (or at least start that process).

Tasks

- Connect to your sexuality.

- Connect to the humanity of others through their needs.

- Connect with yourself beyond your needs.

- As you realize that you are not your needs, but you HAVE needs, don't forget that you still need to attend to your needs. Although they are not you, if you do not attend to them, you can easily fall into spending extra time in this stage.

- Connect with your internal energy and feelings.

- Connect with your money - eliminate the chains of debt servitude from your life.

Stage Four: Others Have Needs Too (I Am My Needs And Others Are Their Needs)

Characteristics

- You see others as individuals with needs of their own; it is not their job to fulfill your needs.

- You practice prioritizing your needs above or below others, and others above or below each other.

- Conscience, guilt, shame, and empathy are now possible and even likely (but can also be faked).

- Your deity is seen as a personified, anthropomorphic, named being who is focused on justice.

- You take religious metaphors, stories and symbolism literally.

Challenges

Although this stage is far less self-centered, it is still focused on your own needs. Financial strain, work stress and other situations that cause scarcity can pull you back to this stage. Fear of loss reigns supreme along with the fear of not having your needs met. There can be a lot of guilt, regret and shame in this stage when reflecting on your past actions. If there are people you need to apologize to, this is a good time to do it.

Tasks

- Connect to others - find ways to help others fulfill their needs.

Connect to yourself...

- Attend to your needs.

- Reflect on your past when you find patterns affecting you today.

- Define your value set / beliefs / ideologies and put it into practice.

Kathryn Colleen, PhD RMT

Connect to your money...

- Solidify your savings engine.

- If you are not yet out of debt, double down on your efforts.

- If you are debt free (good job!), think about the funds you will need in the future and save, save, save.

Stage Five: I Am My Value Set / Ideology / Religion / Beliefs

Characteristics

- You define yourself based on a set of social, moral, political and religious values.

- You have a strong affinity for laws and ethical codes.

- Anything that conflicts with your ideology is ignored or attacked.

- When you see or hear something that conflicts with your ideology, you feel offended or angry.

- You see people with other ideologies as lesser or lower than you, or not human at all, or deserving of bad things.

Challenges

This stage is very challenging because you feel offended and shocked more often than you feel anything else. And just when you think you are beyond this, there is nothing like a good election, news program or religious retreat to pull you back into your ideology. Reading headlines focused on defending and attacking ideologies (political, religious or otherwise) will keep you in this stage far longer than is necessary and will only exacerbate the negatives of this stage.

While it is important to HAVE an ideology just to get through your day and make good choices, it is more important to avoid swinging it at everyone who may feel differently. The biggest challenge in this stage is to have and evolve an ideology but to keep it on the shelf instead of wearing it. Your ideology is there for reference, but you are so much more.

Tasks

Connect to yourself...

- Read about other ideologies - political, social, religious, etc.

- Resist the urge to attack or be rude to others who think differently than you. It may feel justified right now but will be yet one more thing you will have to forgive yourself for in later stages.

- Return to your principles... based on new experiences, do they need to be updated?

- Consider that you HAVE an ideology, but you are so much more.

Connect to others...

- See their humanity through their ideology. (Understand that if they are also in this stage, they may attack or ignore you if you try to sway them. So do not try to sway them, or anyone else. You will be ignored, or attacked and will ultimately not sway anyone.)

Kathryn Colleen, PhD RMT

Stage Six: To Each Their Own (I Am My Ideology And Others Are Their's)

Characteristics

- You can put yourself in other people's shoes and feel what it is like to be them. You can see why they would have a different ideology and what that would be.

- You can consider other ideologies without feeling like yours is being attacked, and without attacking others.

- You reflect on the inconsistencies and complexities of your ideologies and are comfortable with them.

- ...But you think there might be something more; a larger perspective or truth that you are missing.

Challenges

There are far fewer challenges in this stage. You feel much happier with your life. Although you are still defined by your ideology, you are living in a bit of a fantasy world in thinking that your ideology is perfect, or that the inconsistencies are OK. Many adults stay very happily in this stage for life. The treadmill of work, sleep, work, sleep can be a lifelong endeavor and can feel purposeful, if you have work that you love.

If however, you, like most, feel that call to figure out the truth of your self and your life and to design a life of peace, joy, excitement, or anything else you want... Complete this stage and proceed to stage seven.

Tasks

Connect to yourself...

- Return to your own ideology: Detail the cracks, the inconsistencies, hypocrisies and conflicts.

- Look in the mirror and see the person causing 99% of all your problems.

- Forgive and accept yourself as human.

- Connect to your body - Set specific, measurable, and attainable goals with near term milestones.

- Connect to your heart - See that you are worthy of your own love and of the infinite love inside you.

Connect to others...

- See everyone as a reflection of some aspect of yourself.

- Connect to the divine light inside them.

- Forgive and accept others as human.

- Forgive and accept the existence of aspects of society that you previously rejected (groups of people, norms, standards, societal rules, etc).

Stage Seven: Questioning Everything

Characteristics

- In an effort to understand what you are missing, you question everything.

- You realize that happiness cannot be found in the outside world. This is a source of disappointment but also of hope.

- You reject ALL ideologies for now, while you question them.

- Previous doubts become meaningful, actionable questions.

- Sometimes you feel lonely because others are still devoted to their ideologies and they don't understand why you are questioning it.

- You tend to question and undertake this stage in private because of the risk of being alienated from your friends and/or communities.

Challenges

DO NOT MAKE ANY DRASTIC CHANGES IN THIS STAGE! Your best course is to try and not do anything stupid during this phase - no major purchases, no new debt, no job changes, no relationship changes, ... until you make it to Stage Eight and have stability and a clearer mind. Stage Seven is all about tearing down everything that everyone else told you life should be and what you should do, questioning that, and deciding for yourself what you want your self and your life to be. You will want to define that clearly before you make any major changes other than nutrition, exercise, and meditation or prayer. Get through this stage as fast as you can but COMPLETE it so that you will not be pulled back here very often.

This is by far the hardest stage. If you have baggage from your childhood, or past experiences that you have not addressed before, this is where you will have to deal with it. If you can be a bit of a hermit during this stage you may thank yourself later.

This stage is also where you are most likely to be depressed and to feel hopeless or that life is pointless. Existential crises are normal here. Understand that this is a natural part of your development and it will pass with time and effort.

Because of the existential nature of this stage, it is more important than ever to maintain connection to your mind, body, self, others, needs, etc. Keep up your efforts to save money, improve your nutrition, maintain some kind of exercise or movement, and all the other skills you have gathered so far.

Tasks

- Connect to your faith - Understand that questioning your religion is deep exploration that can bring you closer to the divine.

- Question everything... Religious teachings, social standards, political stances, societal norms, life choices, your lifestyle, your work…(Do not try to make others join you in this questioning if they are not ready. This is YOUR journey, not theirs.)

Connect to yourself...

- Practice being mindful of your thoughts and feelings.

- Identify the beliefs about yourself, your life, others and your world put into your mind by your parents, friends, and society. Decide if they are right for you.

- Identify your own behaviors that are sabotaging you (refresh your efforts to find and break negative patterns from Stage Four)

- Dig deep to uncover your own pain from the past and work through it.

- Decide who and what you want to be - more caring? Complete unto yourself? At peace? Quiet your mind and ask how you can achieve these in a healthy way.

- Connect to the infinite silence / divine.

Stage Eight: I Am A Child Of The Universe/ Divine

Characteristics

- You cycle through several belief sets trying to find one that fits and then eventually, instead of rejecting all ideologies, you actively examine them to find what parts are true.

- You see connections and relationships between ideologies.

- You see the interdependent truth at the heart of all ideologies and use THAT to anchor yourself.

- You surrender to not knowing all the answers.

Challenges

In this stage it is now much safer to begin designing your ideal life and making changes. Think through those changes carefully. Take your time so that you might be able to implement your ideal life more efficiently and effectively.

Tasks

- Connect to the universal truth.

- Connect to the Silent Observer.

- Connect to your reality - design your future.

- Connect to your purpose - identify it.

- Connect to others - can you see their truth now? Can you see their heart? Can you see their humanity? Can you see what stage they are in at the moment? Practice!

Stage Nine: I Am A Consciousness Trapped In This Body

Characteristics

- You see religions, people, ideologies, places, and everything as one coherent whole with love at the heart of it all.

- You see that there is no self - you are a consciousness separate from your body and can feel the differences between your physical self and your internal consciousness.

- You do not blame anyone for anything happening in your own life.

- You have a sense of your purpose or mission.

Challenges

The major challenge of this stage is to cultivate presence in the NOW. This moment, not the past or the future. It is a good challenge to have, but harder than it sounds. This stage is a beautiful and purpose-filled place. The joy of acting on your newfound purpose is overwhelming. At the same time, you can feel guilty about this amazing life you are building. You can feel humbled by this gift of insight and connection. But you cannot end the suffering of others by joining them. You CAN, however, offer peace, joy and the example of a path towards a better life. That being said, do not preach. Just live your joy and shine bright.

Tasks

- Connect to this moment.

- Connect to your intuition.

- Connect to your purpose - make a plan.

- Connect to your intellect - gather the skills and knowledge you need to forward your purpose.

- Form a more complete connection to your partner.

Stage Ten: I Am The ONE Consciousness

Characteristics

- You realize that there is only one consciousness. You are an extension of that, as is everyone and everything else.

- You trust your intuition and begin to listen to it more often, training it to tell you what you need to know.

- You live in the moment, not worrying about the future or reliving the past.

Challenges

The biggest challenge in this stage is maintaining the feeling of oneness that you have with everyone and everything. If you try to maintain it, it fades away. You have to not try, and just be in the now, feeling it, flowing in the moment. Be cognizant of how easily you can be pulled back around the cycle into other stages.

Tasks

- Connect to higher wisdom.

- Connect to the oneness and your influence.

- Recognize the triggers that take you out of this stage and make efforts to guard your environment accordingly.

Stage Eleven: I Am The One Consciousness And The Physical Manifestation Simultaneously And There Is No Difference

Characteristics

- You feel the one consciousness, here in this human body, experiencing what it is like to be human - to ignore your humanity would be to miss out on the experience.

- You are matter and energy at the same time. You can consciously choose to experience the moment as either one, or both.

- There is no difference between the energy and the physical.

- You can consciously influence your reality to actively build an ideal life for yourself and alter it as your ideal evolves.

- You live in purpose, peace and joy.

- You connect deeply with yourself, your loved ones, friends and strangers.

- You exude a peace and joy that make people want to be near you.

Challenges

Maintenance, Maintenance, Maintenance. There is a lot to maintain at this point: your needs, your ideology, your experiences, your sense of connectedness and oneness. Once you have tasted this stage, you may find yourself crafting a life for yourself that will let you spend as much time here as possible. That ideal life will look very different for each of us.

As you create space for further (yes, further!) development, you can begin to experiment with actively creating complete connection to yourself, your world, others, etc. Complete connection can help you to return to this stage and stay there as long as possible. In addition to actively creating complete connection, allow your naturally connected state to exist by removing whatever may be covering it up and blocking it.

Actively seek complete connection, and simultaneously relax and allow that complete connection to happen.

Tasks

- Connect to your reality.

- Actively and consciously design and create your ideal life and your ideal self. Live in your purpose with peace and joy.

- Recognize when you are cycling through the stages again. Remember that life will take you around the circle many times but YOU are in control of how much time you spend in each stage.

- Ripples in the water - the strong, consistent signal wins.

- Enjoy your human existence in all of its most basic aspects as well as its more subtle complexities.

- Seek complete connection with yourself, with others, with this moment, your life at large, your money, your purpose, etc.

The Key To Your Journey - CONNECTION

Now that we have the cycle and we understand the stages, the big question is HOW do we move from one stage to another? HOW do we efficiently, effectively and permanently shift perspectives? What is the catalyst that makes someone go from one stage to the next?

The answer to all of those questions is: CONNECTION. Connection means many things. It means being present with, acknowledging, taking ownership of and responsibility for, and forming a deep relationship with the thing in question.

Progressing from one stage to another, or remaining in later stages is a matter of connecting to some aspect of yourself, others, your life, your money, your purpose, your body, your thoughts, ... IN THE RIGHT ORDER.

If you focus on forming and maintaining connection, your evolution through the stages will happen on its own.

But individuals are not evolving in isolation. When you aggregate the stages for all the individuals in a society, or in the whole of humanity, you will find that we, as towns and nations and as a species are evolving along the same stages en mass.

———

Our Evolving Societies

———

Does Society As A Whole, Develop Along The Cycle Just Like An Individual? YES!

We as individuals, traveling our own path, develop along a cycle of social, religious and spiritual growth, revisiting earlier stages and later stages over and over. It stands to reason that we, as a society, also develop and grow the "hive mind" or group-think. At a minimum, when the majority of the population is in a particular stage, we would say that country or region is in that stage.

If you chart any aspect of humanity, from height to age or indeed, stage, you get a "normal" curve. If you chart the current stage of each person in a country or region, you would get a curve that looks something like this.

You can see how more people are in Stage Five than any other stage, in this example. So this would be the dominant stage for this society. But you have a reasonably sized segment of people in stages four and six and some people in stages three and seven, etc.

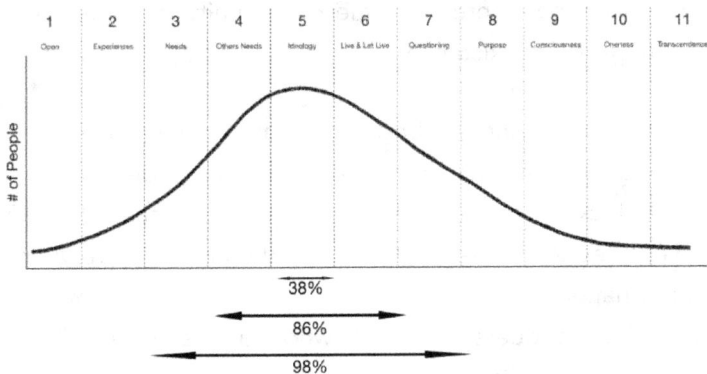

Every society will have some people in each stage. But it's the dominant stage that rules the group-think, vibe, or overall feeling in that country or region. Indeed, you can extract that all the way up to humanity at large. If we could chart the average stage for each person on Earth, we would get a similar curve.

Many thousands of years ago, our days were consumed with finding food, having enough water, a place to sleep, basic safety from predators, warmth and health. At that time, you could say that humanity was in Stage Three: I am my needs and Stage Four: others have needs too. We were largely preoccupied with fulfilling our basic needs and those of our family or tribe. There was little opportunity to contemplate the mysteries of existence.

But at some point, we began to draw on walls and create ideologies to explain what we could not understand, like death, luck, all these other creatures and ourselves. Slowly, we evolved to a society wherein the ideology was everything. Entire nations adopted particular ideologies and drove out, killed or conquered anyone who suggested a different ideology. (The Roman Empire, the crusades, Catholics vs Protestants in England and beyond).

Even today, there are some nations that base themselves on a particular religion, but they are far fewer than in the past, and considered to be somewhat "behind" by western countries. These societies are squarely in Stage Five: I am my ideology. But religious ideology is not all there is. Many western countries are also squarely in Stage Five of the political variety with the majority of the population focused daily on anger and offense at anyone who believes differently.

Go back now to the 1900s where we see an acceleration of further societal development in the United States (as a great but by no means unique example). For a while, we were our political ideology (democracy vs communism). Then, we came to a point where we could see the cracks and inconsistencies in our religious and political ideologies (about 1950), and we wondered if there was something more (Stage Six). By the late 1960s we were rejecting all ideologies (Stage Seven). Leading the way were the hippies and beatniks.

Eventually the post-modernist movement picked up steam in the 1970s to the point of this questioning being taught overtly in public schools (and some private ones). This portion of the population is deeply in Stage Seven (I reject all ideologies) - deconstructing any and every social, political and religious ideology as a human or societal construct and therefore not real and therefore entirely wrong.

Today, at the same time as we have this significant portion of the US population in Stage Seven (I reject all ideologies), we also have the majority of the population in Stage Five (I am my ideology - political and/or religious). But look at how we have evolved as a country and as a species. We have come from MOST people being in Stage Three to Four to MOST people being in Stage Five to Six with a significant portion of the population (enough to dominate the headlines) in Stage Seven. That's GREAT! No, really! Hear me out.

This is great news. First, we, as a society, will have to fully embrace and get through Stage Seven. This is a very dangerous stage. It means rejecting all ideologies, flailing around for a while trying on every possible variant only to meet disappointment when reality shows it to be flawed. THEN, after many bad choices, we as a society will finally get to the point where the majority of the population is in Stage Eight - a society where most people can see the truth at the heart of all ideologies, and most people are focused on their purpose. THAT will be a peaceful society indeed.

Of course, it is a cycle - not a staircase. We, as humanity at large, have had our share of events that have pulled us back to earlier stages only to have to traverse them again, around and around. If you were to plot the timeline of history against the stages of development, you would see us going around and around but in total, spending more and more time with the majority of the population in later and later stages. We will dive into that in detail later. For now, let's focus on what societies look like at each stage.

When we aggregate the characteristics of each stage up to the society level, we can use headlines and overarching social behavior as a marker of that society's stage. Let's take them one by one. See if you can spot your town, your country, and even humanity as we go.

The Stage One Society - Open

Societies evolve along the same cycle of eleven stages that individuals do, because what is a society but a collection of individuals? So how can we identify what stage a society is currently experiencing? Whether it's a town, county, state, province, country or the entirety of humanity, any group of individuals will follow a normal curve. That means, if you plot the number of people in each stage, you will get a graph that looks something like this:

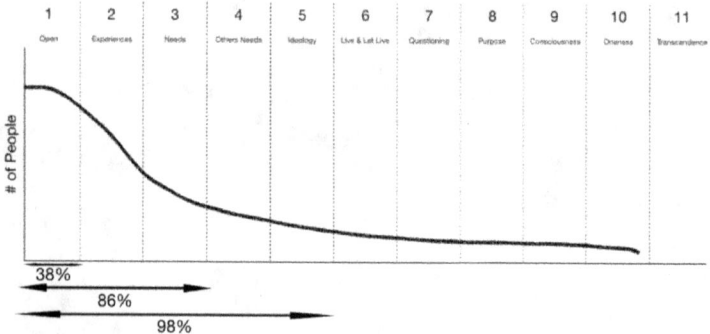

The Stage One society has about 38% of the population in Stage One (open), and another 48% between Stages Two (experiences) and Three (needs), but mostly in Stage Two. Between Stages One, Two and Three you will have about 86% of the total population accounted for. The remaining 14% of the population is scattered between Stages Four through Eleven.

The Stage One society would be one open to the future, experiencing profound beginnings and reassessing its needs. This would be typical of a newly formed country, a nation that recently gained independence, or a people recently freed from oppression. Reeling from the experience, they would be finding new needs, but generally be optimistic about the wide open future.

Headlines would be largely optimistic and focused on planning within the new government or leadership, with a scattering of human interest stories on what people experienced prior to this era, and what they feel they need now.

The Stage Two Society - Experiences

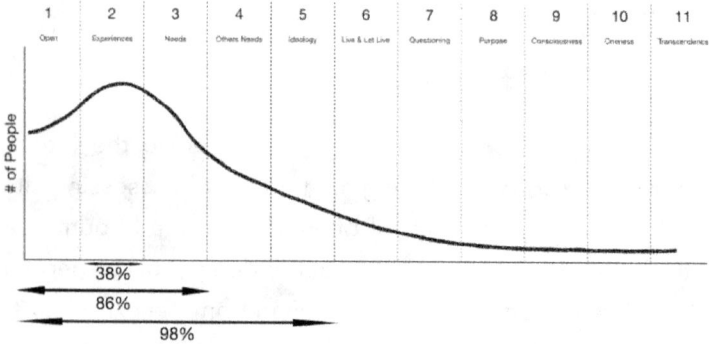

In the Stage Two society, we see a shift to having 38% of the population in Stage Two, detaching from and processing experiences. You would have approximately 24% in Stage One (open) and another 24% in Stage Three (needs). The remaining 14% are scattered between Stages Four through Eleven.

This society would have a larger focus on their own needs, if only they could stop reliving their recent experiences over and over. The optimistic tone of the Stage One society fades a little, as calls for fulfilling needs become louder. Some would take this as a sign that their leadership has failed, but in reality, the society is evolving right on schedule.

Headlines in this stage will focus on recent experiences and, secondarily, on needs not being fulfilled and a bit of latent optimism about the future.

This society is rebuilding itself as the world watches. This stage is typical of locations that are facing rebuilding after natural disasters. The threat was short lived and now gone and there is hope for recovery. Leaders in the Stage Two society should be careful to understand and fulfill new and unmet needs quickly to avoid a full blown Stage Three society, which can be challenging at best and violent at worst.

The Stage Three Society - Needs

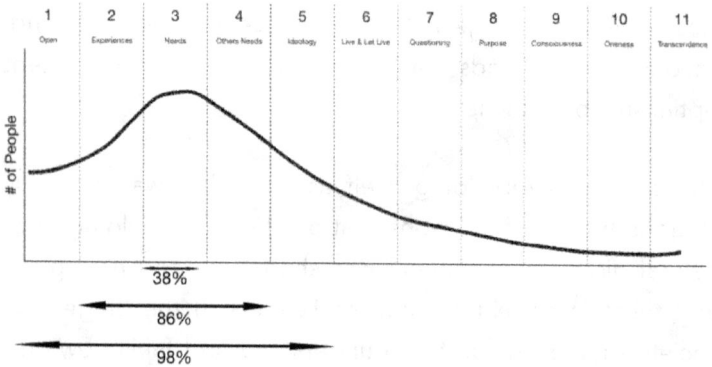

In this example, we would say this particular country is in Stage Three, because there are more people in Stage Three than in any other stage. But that doesn't mean that EVERYONE in that country is in Stage Three. In every society, you will have some people in each stage. The beauty of the normal curve is that it gives you a pretty good estimate of what percent of the population is in each stage.

So if, like this example, we have a peak in Stage Three, we can see that it is likely that 38% of the population is in Stage

Three and focused on their own needs. And if we take Stages Two through Four all together, we would have about 86% of the population accounted for. That puts about 24% of the population in Stage Two and another 24% in Stage Four.

This is a typical scenario for third world nations as well as those recovering from war, pandemic or natural disaster, if needs are not met swiftly. In these countries, a portion of the population is simply stunned by what has happened or what is currently happening (experiences), a larger portion is focused on survival needs, and another portion is focused on helping others. The remaining 14% of the population is scattered between Stages One and Five through Eleven.

Societies in this stage are dominated by a fear of unmet needs - not enough money, food, water, and so forth. If needs are unmet for too long, need becomes desperation. Desperate people do desperate things. Fear of unmet needs leads to increased crime, mostly theft. If needs continue to be unmet, crime turns to rioting and other forms of violence.

This is incredibly frustrating to the 24% of the population focused on the needs of others, as crime and violence only exacerbate the unmet needs. Meanwhile, that same crime and violence perpetuate the portion of the population stuck in their experiences, by adding new major experiences like increasing crime or violence in their neighborhoods.

Leaders in a Stage Three society should be focused not only on meeting needs quickly, but getting the population at large focused on the needs of others, thereby moving the whole society to Stage Four.

I wish I could say that moving the society to Stage Four solves all your problems, but Stage Four societies have a new set of challenges to deal with.

The Stage Four Society - The Needs Of Others

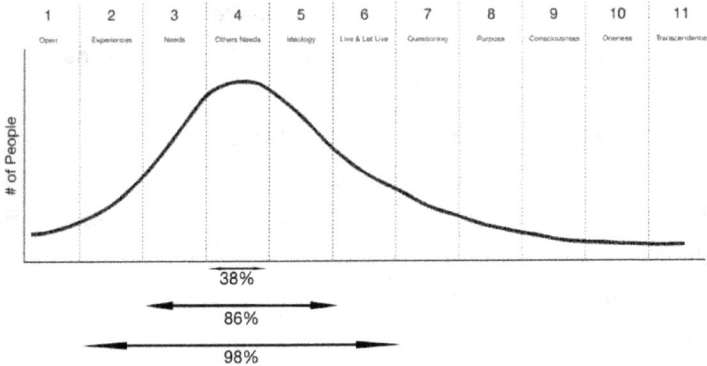

In the Stage Four society, 76% of the population has their needs met to the point that they are not in fear of those needs not being met. They do not fear a lack of food, water, shelter, clothing, safety and so on. 24% of the population would still be grappling with those needs. 38% of the population would be focused now on the needs of others, and 24% would have moved forward to being ruled by their ideologies, political or otherwise. The remaining 14% would be scattered between Stage One and Two and Stages Six through Eleven.

While the dominant stage is Stage Four, focused on the needs of others, you will not have as peaceful and altruistic a society as you might think. In this society, you have a combined 48% in Stage Three and Stage Five. These are two very challenging stages. Those in Stage Three have needs that have gone unmet for some time now, leading to desperation. Those in Stage Five, are soaking in anger and offense at any differing opinions and flinging their beliefs at anyone and everyone, signaling to the whole nation how right they are, and how wrong everyone else is.

It is a society ultimately overtaken by fear and anger as much as it is by altruism. The negative emotions of fear and anger account for more of the population than caring and altruism. Therefore, negative emotions dominate the scene. Headlines would focus in almost equal parts on stories of unmet needs, stories of charity work, and stories about political infighting.

Because of the increase in altruism within this society, you might feel that they are making progress past their previous crime-ridden Stage Three status. You would be right. But it might be hard to see. In the Stage Four society, although the number of people with unmet needs are fewer, they are more desperate and therefore more violent. What might have been thousands protesting and rising theft in the last stage, is now hundreds rioting, burning and looting and a prominent few dozen bent on murder, just waiting for an excuse.

On the bright side, with over a third working for the needs of others, those needs will soon be met and the violence will largely subside, leading even more of the population into Stage Four, Stage Five, and Stage Six.

The Stage Five Society - Ideology

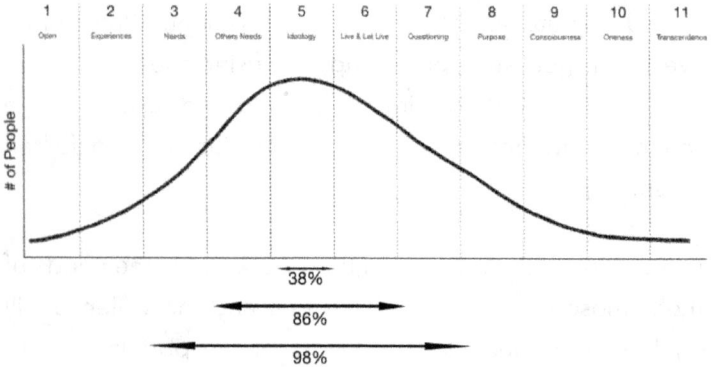

A country in Stage Five would look something like this. This would include most first world countries today and several developing nations with religious governments. In these societies, you again see three main portions of the population.

Here you would have roughly 24% in Stage Four, largely focused on the needs of others, 38% in Stage Five, feeling offended and angry and constantly defending their ideology while berating others, and 24% in Stage Six just trying to live their lives. The remaining 14% of the population is scattered between Stages One through Three and Stages Seven Through Eleven.

Not surprisingly, societies in Stage Five, dominated by ideologies, look like a real mess. Headlines will say it's the end of the world and everyone will feel like their society is falling apart. The majority of news articles will focus on ideology (political or religious), people of one ideology bashing people of an opposing ideology, and the ensuing divisiveness. In fact, headlines may reflect the population percentages with some portion of headlines discussing good deeds done by those attending to the needs of others, people in great need, people questioning everything, and a few spiritual people talking about connection.

With a now significant portion (24%) of the population in Stage Six (live and let live, or passive ideology), there is a lot less overt violence, but a lot more verbal ugliness, mostly from the dominant percentage of people in Stage Five. The 24% of the population focused on the needs of others (Stage Four) is less than before, but still significant enough to be doing a lot of good.

With a combined 48% in Stage Four and Stage Six, you have positive emotions, or at least a combination of caring and free-wheeling apathy, tamping down the effect of the 38% in Stage Five feeling anger and offense. Things will seem overall better than when this society was in Stage Four. Violence is subsiding, but political infighting is prominent. We have traded in physical violence for verbal fights, and physical murder for "cancel culture" that ruins careers and finances.

The Stage Six Society - Live And Let Live

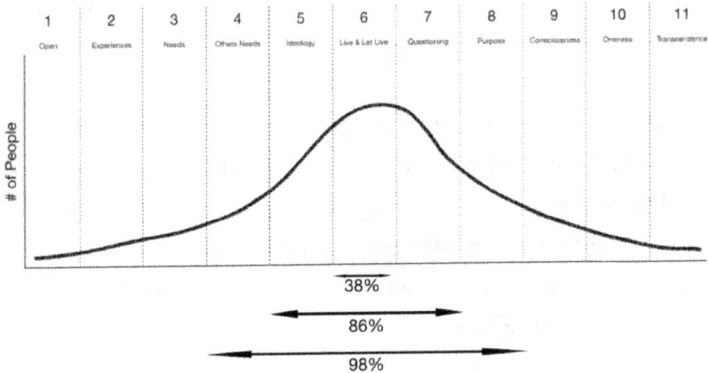

1	2	3	4	5	6	7	8	9	10	11
Open	Experiences	Needs	Others Needs	Ideology	Live & Let Live	Questioning	Purpose	Consciousness	Oneness	Transcendence

# of People

38%

86%

98%

A Stage Six society, focused just one stage over would be quite a bit different. In these societies, you have a large number of people (38%) happy to just live and let live. You now have just 24% in Stage Five, focused on their ideologies. This is enough to cause a lot of lashing out online, but the headlines in these countries would not tend to lead with ideological divisiveness.

Although there would still be a decent portion of headlines focused on who said what about which political or religious issue, the majority of headlines would become more about

73

actual happenings, with a portion of headlines devoted to disillusionment with status quo, innovation and new ideas. This disillusionment and innovation comes from the 24% of the population in Stage Seven.

Stage Seven is an interesting stage. The first time an individual or society encounters Stage Seven, it is all disillusionment; the dark night of the soul. But when we encounter this stage later on in subsequent trips through the cycle, it takes on a flavor of innovation and becomes, ultimately, a lot of fun.

So while this 24% of the population visits Stage Seven, we get a taste of what is to come. Is it disillusionment and depression or will it be innovation and independent thinking?

If the Stage Seven portion of the population is experiencing disillusionment and depression, then you have, combined with the Stage Five portion of the population, a larger percent experiencing negative emotions than the moderately happy emotions of Stage Six. The combined disillusionment plus anger and offense can make the overall society feel on the verge of something bad. But ultimately, questioning is good for any society long term.

If the Stage Seven portion of the population is experiencing innovation, instead, the overall feel of this Stage Six society can be quite positive as they sit back and wait for new, better ideas.

The Stage Seven Society - Questioning Everything

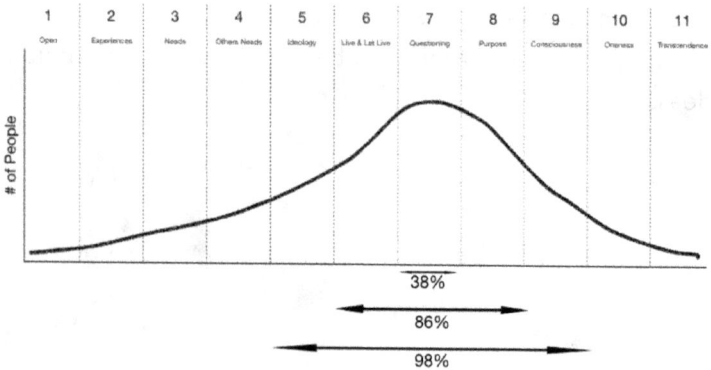

Some developed nations have seen Stage Seven before. It looks like revolution - political, social, technological or cultural. In fact, that is the order you would tend to see in any given country. The first time a society encounters Stage Seven typically results in political revolution - a major shift in structure. If the new choice of structure was a bad one, you might see another political revolution later.

Once a better structure is in place, subsequent trips through Stage Seven will look like next a social revolution (such as the women's suffrage movement or the American civil rights movement) and then a series of cultural revolutions driven by significant technological innovation, or sometimes ideological choices.

We can think of a number of countries that have seen Stage Seven several times. So why do they seem to be in Stage Five now? It's a cycle. That is key. Individuals and societies alike all traverse the cycle. Elections and societal shifts can pull a population back around to Stage Five just as war or pandemic can pull them back around to Stage Three.

No society, however, is solely one stage. In the Stage Seven society, while we have a dominant 38% in Stage Seven, we also have 24% in Stage Six (live and let live) and another 24% in Stage Eight (purpose). Regardless of whether this society's Stage Seven is disillusionment or innovation, a full 48% of the population is feeling pretty great, focused on living their own lives and pursuing their purpose. When a society is experiencing an innovative Stage Seven, life is good and positive indeed.

Headlines in a Stage Seven society will focus on questioning the status quo, calling for change, discussing new discoveries and innovations, and celebrating independent thought. Smaller portions of headlines will detail purpose-driven individuals and methods for finding your own purpose.

One critical note is that a negative Stage Seven in the form of disillusionment will see calls for significant change, but suppression of independent thought, while a positive Stage Seven in the form of innovation will celebrate independent thought while change happens naturally through innovative approaches. The first is based in questioning through fear and ideology and the second is based in an open and curious style of questioning that can be almost fun and exciting.

The Stage Eight Society - Purpose

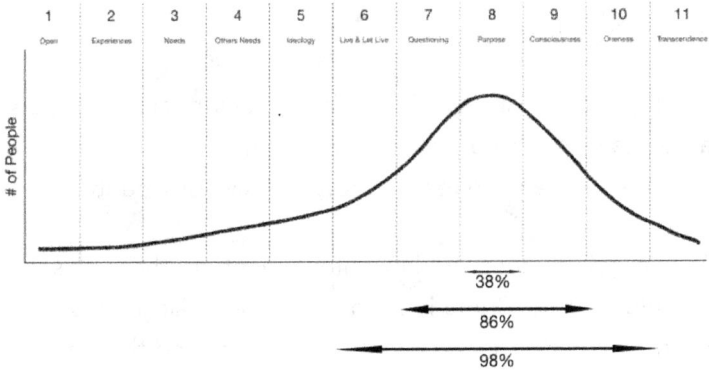

1	2	3	4	5	6	7	8	9	10	11
Open	Experiences	Needs	Others Needs	Ideology	Live & Let Live	Questioning	Purpose	Consciousness	Oneness	Transcendence

38%
86%
98%

So what happens when we eventually get to a society where the peak is in Stage Eight?

The Stage Eight society is one of incredible productivity, joy, and passion. You have about 38% of the population reveling in their purpose-driven efforts; doing what they were born to do and loving it. That means they are doing it very well. The 24% of the population in Stage Seven will be largely the innovation type, rather than the disillusionment type. That only feeds purpose-driven action even further. And then there are 24% of the population in Stage Nine, beginning to explore their own consciousness. This is an incredibly peaceful stage, marked by increased intuition and patience. What a great mix!

For the economists out there, that means quality products, large scale innovation, new markets and ideas and people excited to make them real. In short: massive prosperity.

For the government and law enforcement out there, this is a peaceful society. Crime is at an all time low. Altruism is at an all time high. People are nice to each other, and those few in Stage Three with unmet needs are more than attended to by the larger number of people in Stages Four and Eight. The Stage Five population is now so small that any negative effect is neutralized.

Headlines in a Stage Eight society will be largely positive, focusing on purpose-driven companies and individuals, new innovations, and the latest discoveries in the science of consciousness.

And it only gets better from there.

The Stage Nine Through Eleven Society - Consciousness, Oneness And Transcendence

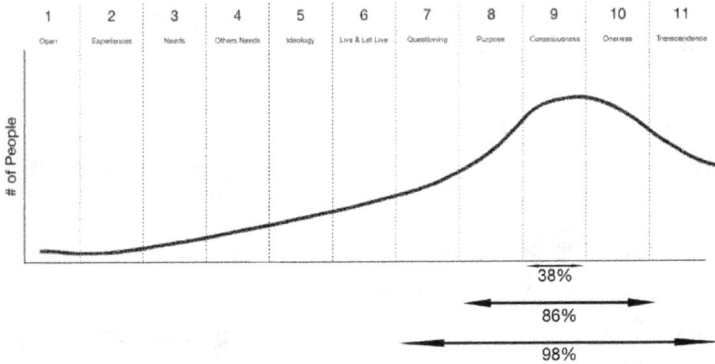

The Stage Nine society would have 38% of the population focused on their own consciousness, 24% on their purpose-driven efforts and another 24% on oneness. The remaining 14% would be scattered between Stages One through Seven and Stage Eleven.

To my knowledge, no society on Earth has ever even so much as touched the edge of such a society. So I will have to guess at what it might look like. Let's give it a try. Consciousness research would be a mainstay of the scientific community. With so much focus on oneness and purpose, it would be a very peaceful and prosperous society. Headlines would focus on issues related to consciousness, oneness and purpose.

But we might also see a movement away from the traditional measures of success such as cars, houses and other status symbols. People in these later stages tend to strive instead for internal rewards, favoring a more minimalist lifestyle. This could cause a shift in economies as rampant consumerism is replaced with a more toned down variant. Products and services that support inner work such as meditation, exploring states of consciousness and brainwave activity will proliferate and become commonplace in homes. We might see a shift to more local and in-person consumption and events as connection becomes a larger priority.

As this society shifts further into Stages Ten and Eleven, we see larger percentages of people focused on oneness and transcendence. These are profound experiences. The thing is, this is a cycle, not a staircase. Although the example graphs show the stages as a straight line across the page, there is no wall after Stage Eleven.

What happens is that profound experiences change us. We must then process the experience. The next thing you know we are right back in Stage One and Stage Two, processing and detaching from the profound experiences of Stage Eleven. Within that deep personal change is often a new set of needs, drawing us back to Stage Three to address them. And around the cycle we go.

32 Steps

——

Our Evolving Humanity

Through Time

——

Human History Through The Stages

Let's turn our attention now to the larger picture of the whole of humanity. Humanity has been evolving through the cycle of development since the beginning. If you were to plot major eras on the cycle, you would see how we seem to oscillate forward and backwards, but overall, we are moving to the right. Taken in the context of a cycle, we go around and around, but spend more and more time in later stages.

We had to learn through the Stone Age and other early eras to process our experiences and meet our basic needs. As ideologies took over, we as a species moved into Stage Five, with it the violence of the Middle Ages and later the questioning of the Protestant Reformation. Progress forward was seen over and over through our history, punctuated by war, plague and economic depressions which moved us seemingly backwards. We will discuss that more later. For now, notice how we keep moving forward, despite periodic setbacks.

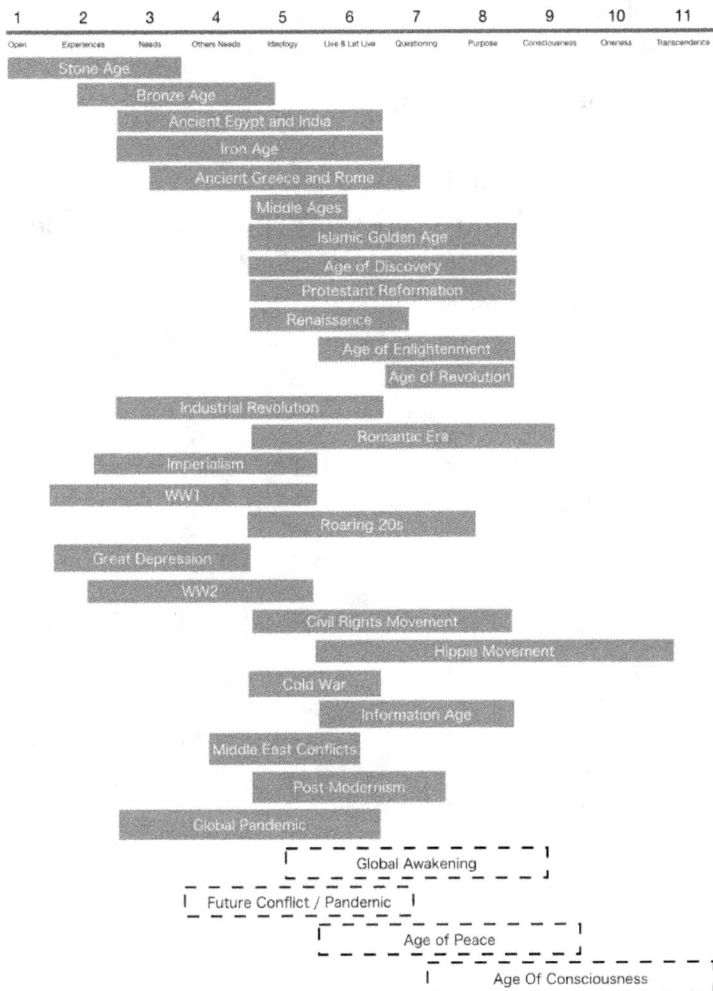

1	2	3	4	5	6	7	8	9	10	11
Open	Experiences	Needs	Others Needs	Ideology	Live & Let Live	Questioning	Purpose	Consciousness	Oneness	Transcendence

Stone Age
Bronze Age
Ancient Egypt and India
Iron Age
Ancient Greece and Rome
Middle Ages
Islamic Golden Age
Age of Discovery
Protestant Reformation
Renaissance
Age of Enlightenment
Age of Revolution
Industrial Revolution
Romantic Era
Imperialism
WW1
Roaring 20s
Great Depression
WW2
Civil Rights Movement
Hippie Movement
Cold War
Information Age
Middle East Conflicts
Post-Modernism
Global Pandemic
Global Awakening
Future Conflict / Pandemic
Age of Peace
Age Of Consciousness

Forward movement, as we have seen at the society level, is not always happy and comfortable. In fact, it can be quite uncomfortable, and outright violent. But every stage is necessary. Evolution forward often brings new experiences, new technologies, new ways of living and therefore new needs that need to be processed, recognized and filled. What worked before doesn't work anymore. Change is called for and we find ourselves in Stage Seven, questioning and changing the status quo. It's uncomfortable and often stressful.

But looking forward, we can see that there are beautiful days ahead if only we can get through our growing pains.

Stepping "Backwards"

So what pulls us backwards? War, pandemic and economic disaster... but mostly war.

Look at all the times we went "backwards" as a species. War causes all involved to be pulled back around to Stage Three (I am my needs). It's about survival and survival is all those involved can focus on. It's hard to focus on concepts of the divine and questioning ideas when you don't know if you or your loved ones might make it through the day. War, in this way, delays the progress of humanity at large, but it does not ultimately prevent it.

And of course, we would be remiss if we didn't discuss the recent global pandemic of 2019-2020. Never before has the entirety of humanity been engulfed simultaneously in the same experience. If you watched closely, you would see the stages in action.

At first, people were afraid. What is this? Am I in danger? Fear of death dominated headlines and private conversations alike. Just a few months prior we were enjoying an economic boom and a hard core Stage Seven, on path for a purpose-filled Stage Eight society within 5-10 years. And then... wham! We were collectively, worldwide, in a fear-filled Stage Three, seeking only to preserve our own survival.

We shut everything down in a fearful bid to hide from the threat. Then the consequences, intended and unintended, arose. Our physical survival and subsequently our individual economic survival was called into question. Isolated and afraid, we disconnected from each other. Suicide and depression rates increased and our mental survival was now threatened.

The sheer magnitude and strangeness of the experience itself caused many to become stuck in Stage Two simply trying to process what was happening, while most lived in fear and isolation, and a third portion focused on the needs of others. Headlines were fearful and survival focused.

Then, about a month into it, something changed. Headlines started to show people singing from their balconies, packing lunches for truckers and cheering on medical professionals. We started to focus on others. We had moved from Stage

Three to Stage Four. This lasted for a while and then the political blame game began... Stage Five. Headlines went from singing on the balconies to who blamed what politician for the next issue.

Meanwhile, it was an election season in some countries leading a vast majority of their citizens straight into hard core Stage Five, wallowing in their ideologies. Political ideologies now included aspects of the pandemic such as being for or against masks and for or against lockdowns of various types, as well as more typical national issues. Each party took up positions and their voting bases tagged along, with both sides vehemently defending their platforms and belittling anyone who opposed.

Meanwhile, unmet needs piled up in the form of overdue rent and lack of income from jobs lost in the shutdown. Need turned to desperation and large scale protests became small scale riots and violence. Sound familiar? This living example of a society evolving through the stages could not be more textbook in its path.

32 Steps

1	2	3	4	5	6	7	8	9	10	11
Open	Experiences	Needs	Others Needs	Ideology	Live & Let Live	Questioning	Purpose	Consciousness	Oneness	Transcendence

Stone Age

Bronze Age

Ancient Egypt and India

Iron Age

Ancient Greece and Rome

Middle Ages

Islamic Golden Age

Age of Discovery

Protestant Reformation

Renaissance

Age of Enlightenment

Age of Revolution

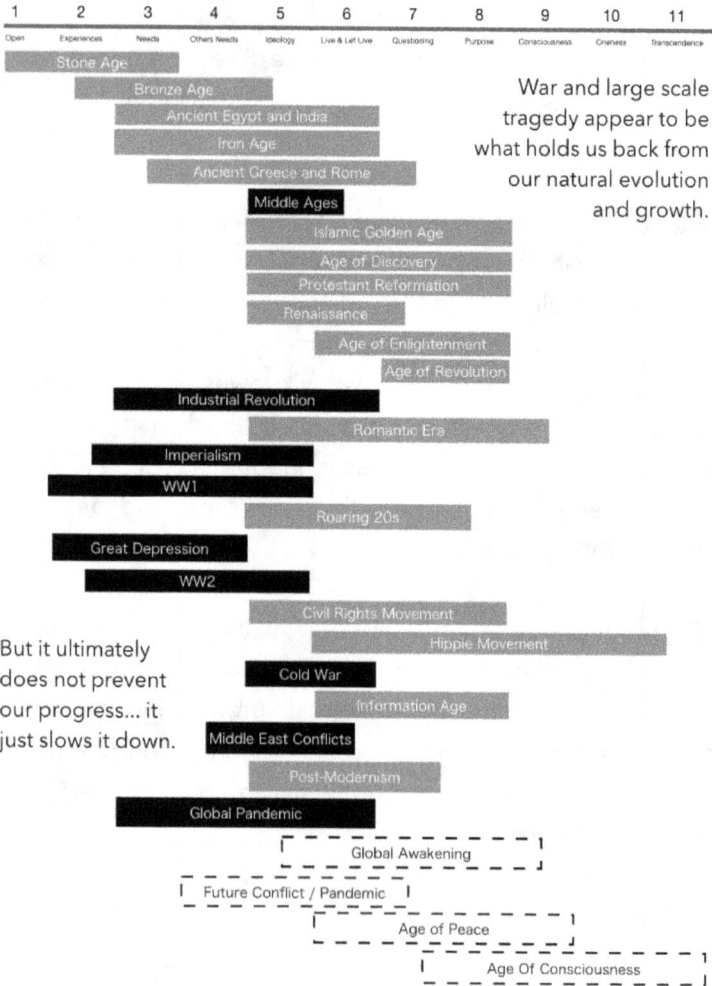

War and large scale tragedy appear to be what holds us back from our natural evolution and growth.

Industrial Revolution

Romantic Era

Imperialism

WW1

Roaring 20s

Great Depression

WW2

Civil Rights Movement

Hippie Movement

But it ultimately does not prevent our progress... it just slows it down.

Cold War

Information Age

Middle East Conflicts

Post-Modernism

Global Pandemic

Global Awakening

Future Conflict / Pandemic

Age of Peace

Age Of Consciousness

And all of this has taken place in less than 8 months. That is phenomenal. Let me explain. Each major turn around the cycle for humanity has taken its time. But each turn around seems to be taking less and less time. What was hundreds of years to recover from a setback like war, plague or famine, became tens of years, and then a year or two and now we are looking at less than a year for this particular example.

This is important, because we would like to have an idea of not only where we go from here, but how long it will take to get there.

Exponential Progress

Our progress is exponential! Moving from one stage to another used to take thousands of years, then hundreds of years, then tens of years. We are moving forward at an exponential pace. We have the potential to easily see the next steps very soon indeed.

At our current pace, we are starting to race back from a pandemic-induced Stage Three, to our previous Stage Five to Six within months to a year. That is an amazing recovery in terms of regaining our previous psychology. So, although setbacks seem to come on quickly, so does recovery.

Why does this happen? Why is it that we go farther faster, over time? We go farther faster over time because these "setbacks" are not setbacks at all. We have never gone backwards, we have only gone forward, around the cycle again, and therefore, having seen these early stages before, we handle them better and move ourselves along more efficiently. As they say, this isn't our first rodeo.

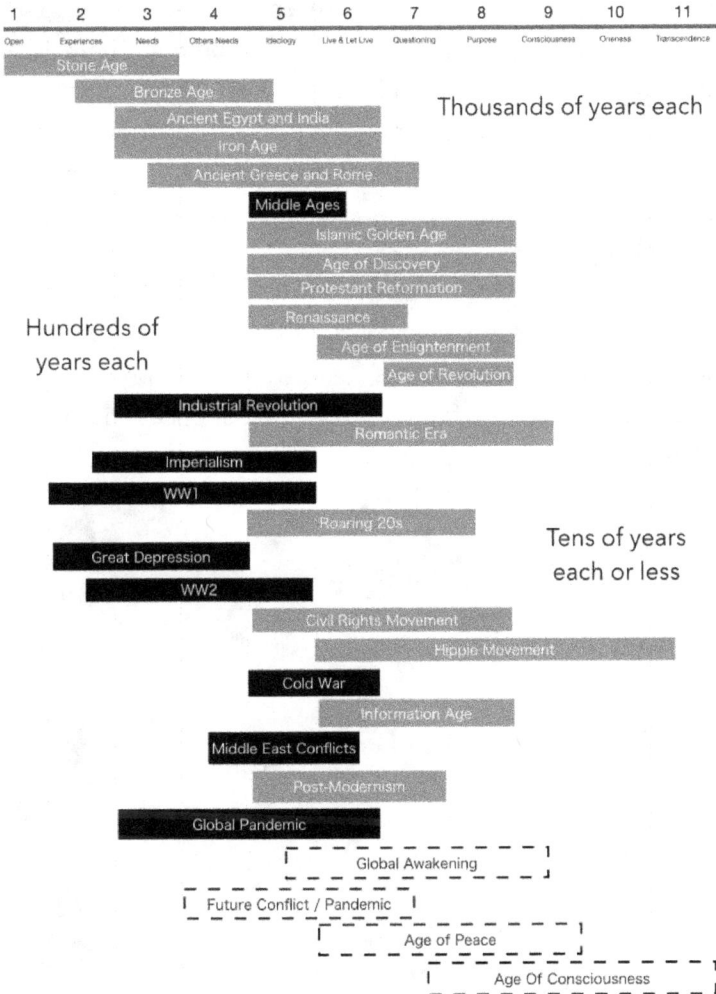

Each time you revisit early, more challenging stages, it is scary, but not quite so scary as it was before. There is a collective human memory that tells us we will ultimately be OK. There is always another end of the world to look forward to. So we move on and return more quickly to the indulgence of our near term past; in this case, a hearty Stage Five with lots of juicy political infighting.

The more interesting question is.... where we will go from here. Profound experiences tend to shock people into awakening. And profound global experiences have the potential for global awakening.

Kathryn Colleen, PhD RMT

———

Where We Will Go

From Here

———

Global Awakening

Prior to the events of 2019-2020 we, as a collective humanity, were on a path to later stages. Many western societies were in Stage Five or Stage Six, and had seen several rounds of Stage Seven before, lending lots of innovation to the mix.

The experience of a global pandemic, or rather the experience of our global reaction to that pandemic (shutdowns, masks, and general panic) is a major life experience. People alive today will be telling their great-grandchildren stories about the great global pandemic of 2019-2020.

Experiences change people. Big experiences change people in big ways. And major experiences that force you to confront your mortality will cause you to awaken and start asking the big questions... what are we doing? Is this what I wanted from life? Why am I here, anyway? What do I want my life to be? What is freedom? What is it to feel safe? And so many more.

Our collective reaction to this particular pandemic not only forced the entirety of humanity to face its mortality, but it completely upended life as we knew it and put a large percentage of humanity on time out for months of reflection. If this does not lead to global awakening, I don't know what will.

Awakening is essentially a midlife crisis. You enter a deep Stage Seven and begin to question EVERYTHING from your career choices to relationships, future, spirituality and more. For some, this will feel like disillusionment and depression while you seek answers. For others who have seen the dark night of the soul before, it could look like a very fun time designing a new life for your yourself, and every experience between.

At scale, this would look like humanity at large in Stage Seven, which includes significant portions of the population in Stage Six (live and let live) and Stage Eight (purpose). It's a really good thing, because it ultimately leads to a Stage Eight society and that is a very happy and peaceful world.

But meanwhile, things are going to get uncomfortable as large portions of humanity make major changes. We can expect major changes to how parents choose to educate their children, how we choose to work, the professions we choose, where we seek to live and what we want daily life to look like. Many individuals making major changes simultaneously will collapse some industries and create new ones in short order. There is opportunity here, if we are willing to seek it.

The key will be to let go of the past and allow room for a new and improved future.

Future Conflict / Pandemic

But let's not be naive. We are not likely to simply run forward toward unified bliss unabated. Before we reach that golden time of a Stage Eight society, there is sure to be another break in the momentum that seems to pull us back.

Among all of this questioning everything will be an opportunistic few still in Stage Three or Stage Five who will lash out at the evolving change with violent response. OR, among those who really should learn and change, there will be some who go back to sleep and learn nothing, sprouting yet another global pandemic later on. Some kind of conflict or some kind of disease, or both, are unavoidable.

But here is the neat thing. We have seen wars and conflict before and they grow shorter and less deadly over time. The next conflict will therefore be likely short-lived and quickly recovered from. And we have now seen global pandemic at scale. The next time global pandemic strikes, we will be prepared with the lessons of the recent past: what worked, what didn't work, what worked but wasn't ultimately worth it, and what else we might have tried. Among all of those lessons will be that it was not, in the end, worthy of fear. Action, yes. Fear, no. The next pandemic will simply not be as frightening. We will be smarter, and better prepared and therefore calmer, knowing that this too shall pass.

A calmer humanity will not delve as deeply into Stage Two or Stage Three, because the experience will not be novel and the fear will not be overwhelming. We will be more likely to snap straight into Stage Four and focus on others. We will recover even more quickly. One year might look like a few months. And we will be back on track again.

But back on track to what? To a Stage Eight society... and the age of peace.

The Age Of Peace

The Age of Peace would see the overwhelming majority of humanity in Stages Seven through Nine. This would be what we call a Stage Eight society, where there are more people in Stage Eight than in any other stage, but significant portions of the population in Stage Seven and Stage Nine. It is a largely peaceful and economically prosperous society, marked by innovation, purpose-driven work, and a focus on understanding consciousness.

You can see the foundations of that society peeking out around the corners of our western world before the 2019-2020 pandemic. Innovation is popular and encouraged within the technology sector (that's a good start), the idea of a purpose-driven life and work model is gaining popularity, and the medical profession is beginning to research consciousness as a mainstream area of study.

It would seem that the age of peace has begun. However, at the moment, there are too many people in Stages Three to Six to allow innovation, purpose-driven work and understanding of consciousness to become the MAIN thing across even western society. But we will get there soon enough.

So what does that look like? The Age of Peace would look like a society where innovation is encouraged and expected in ALL sectors and industries, where career counseling and education focuses on helping people find their purpose and their passion, and crafting a career from that, rather than the other way around, and where the study of consciousness is so mainstream that it is part of Biology and Psychology classes at the High School level.

Innovation in the technology and medical sectors is a great start. In the Age of Peace, we will see innovation encouraged in every sector from government and safety to education, events, restaurants and everything between. Government and innovation are not two words that have ever been seen together, but it will come along.

In the education sector, major changes would be seen that adapt education away from older manufacturing age models towards purpose-driven models. Purpose-driven models will be prioritized that allow students to explore independent interests early on and hone in on what lights them up, not just what everyone else says is a good idea. Imagine if, by the time you reach eighteen, you know the industry that excites you the most and have already had enough experience in that industry to know how you might make a living and love your work at the same time.

In some schools in the United States, you can do that right now by simply taking some interesting electives, but such programs will become more the norm rather than the exception. Focus on preparing for college will evolve into preparing for life and finding your purpose in the context of career.

Consciousness research, today a budding field ripe for discovery, will see a boom in funding and therefore results. The focus on consciousness as a life priority will also lead to significant changes in how we teach high school students about their minds, their psychology and their overall development. In other words, textbooks will catch up with today's understanding.

I call this the Age of Peace, not because there is never any conflict, but because there is so little that it is effectively neutralized. The overwhelming majority of humanity in this age is far too interested in innovation, purpose-driven work and exploration of consciousness to cause any trouble to anyone else. It will be a beautiful time indeed.

The Age Of Consciousness

The Age of Consciousness would come next. This will be a society where the overwhelming majority of people are in Stages Eight through Eleven, with an emphasis on Stages Nine and Ten. This type of society is focused on the wisdom of intuition, a more natural connection with the divine, and a mainstreaming of energy work.

Intuition is, even today considered important, but we still base our decisions largely on data and "provable fact". In the Age of Consciousness, intuition will take priority, while data and fact will be used to back it up. Intuition will be taught in schools with the focus on honing your intuitive skills at an early age. We see the early beginnings of this in the emotional intelligence training that is becoming popular in business circles.

As society at large craves a deeper and more natural connection to the divine, we may see an evolution of religion away from organized, brick and mortar based hierarchies. At first, organized religion will be avoided, or even rejected by many in a bid for more natural, internal connection to the divine. This modern exodus has already begun in most western countries and was accelerated by shutting down churches during the global pandemic. Seeing their revenues drop, many organized religions will eventually innovate new ways to help their devotees find that natural, internal connection to the divine while maintaining their original sacred texts, but not their original hierarchies. Such an evolution of organized religion to something that might be better described as distributed religion will have an interesting effect... the blending of many religions within a single household.

When in these later stages, the truth at the heart of all religions is far more important than the differences. You might see, for example, a single family incorporate aspects of several different religions into their daily lives. This is commonplace in many parts of Asia today, where many families blend aspects of Buddhism, Taoism and Confucianism for a tailored, meaningful connection to the divine. In the Age of Consciousness, I don't think it will be strange to see aspects of Christianity, Islam, and Buddhism, for example, used within the same family for tailored, meaningful transitions and rights of passage. That seems a terribly long way off right now, but when the time comes, it will be very natural.

Energy work, in its many forms, is already mainstream in some cultures. In Eastern cultures and in parts of South America, energy work for healing of all manner of emotional and physical ailments is not just common, it is expected. Energy work in the form of Reiki, a Japanese tradition, was first introduced to the western world in the 1950s and 1960s, and has since grown in popularity. There are, as of this writing, over a million Reiki practitioners worldwide, and over one hundred thousand masters (including myself). At this moment, many hospitals have incorporated Reiki energy work programs using volunteer practitioners who assist those recovering from surgery, at end of life, or even at the beginning of life. It is not so far fetched that we would see this trend continue to increase to the point of seeing energy work fully incorporated into western medicine and daily life, and to see it as a point of research for better understanding.

We see the beginnings of the Age of Consciousness all around us in the western world, and perhaps even more so in the Eastern world. While the Age of Peace will be a time of looking inward, the Age of Consciousness will be a time of looking upward.

Each of these future ages will have its share of challenges and setbacks. But as we have seen in our own history to date, challenges are becoming easier, recoveries are faster, and progress forward is exponential.

———

Getting There

———

Is It Possible To Move Entire Societies Into Another Stage? Yes. But Be Ethical About It.

We know that societies, whether a town, a state or an entire country, evolve through the same stages of development that individuals do - because a society is just a collection of individuals. At any one time, if you mapped out the population by stage, it would look like a normal curve that peaked at that society's primary stage.

If you wanted to move that peak to another stage intentionally, I believe you could do that. But before I tell you how to do that, let's discuss the ethics of doing something like that.

Suppose a society was in Stage Three - such as a developing nation - and you wanted to move them to Stage Six - a more developed and more peaceful nation. That's a nice idea. Not too many people would see a problem with that. But suppose instead that you intentionally moved a society to Stage Seven (questioning everything). This would be incredibly destabilizing and irresponsible. You would have a full 38% of the population protesting, rebelling, and/or so depressed that they could not function. Not cool.

Essentially, if a society is in a rough stage like Three, Five or Seven, you are doing them a favor to help them get past it to a more pleasant stage. But if you intentionally move a society to one of these rough stages where negative emotions dominate and problems abound, then I cannot condone that. Don't do that.

And be aware that, you can move a society temporarily to a higher stage directly, but they won't stay there very long. They will stay only as long as you continue the onerously heavy work to focus them there. A permanent shift to a higher stage requires stepping through each stage along the way and completing it.

So if a society is in Stage Three, and you want to move them to Stage Eight, that means you will have to walk them through Stages Four through Seven. You will have to competently shepherd them through all of those stages, including Stages Five and Seven. If you don't do that correctly, they could get stuck and getting stuck makes things infinitely worse. Because getting stuck in any stage amplifies the effects of that stage. Getting stuck in a stage full of negative emotions does a lot of damage and can result in criminal and otherwise dangerous personalities.

Now that I have scared you away from trying to influence an entire society, let's talk about how to do it. There are two ways to do it: temporarily or permanently.

To temporarily shift a society to a given stage, you would, in theory, simply inundate them with the questions and signals relevant to that stage. I can imagine several ways to do that. I bet you can too. I will not detail that here.

The only time this temporary shift might not work is if you are trying to shift a Stage Three society too far away from Stage Three for too long. For those societies focused on the needs of survival, you will not get a major shift, or a long term shift, but you could get a shift to Stage Four (others) for a few months. Ultimately, you will have to help them meet their needs in order to get a larger shift.

Kathryn Colleen, PhD RMT

For other societies in Stage Four and higher, you could exact a larger temporary shift, for example from Stage Five (ideology) to Stage Eight (purpose) for a few months at a time. But it will not be sustainable, because they did not adequately address the stages between.

To move a society to a previous stage from where they are now, you will have to provide an appropriate trigger, at scale, based on the stage you want. For example, if a society is currently in Stage Five (ideology), and you want to move them to Stage Four (others), that is a step backwards and will require intense focus on the needs of others, which people in Stage Five do not worry too much about. You would have to take them back to Stage Three, and then move them forward to Stage Four from there. But taking people back to Stage Three, or backwards at all, is a really mean thing to do. Don't do that. Move them forward instead.

To move a society to another Stage with more permanent results, you will need to help them address each stage in turn along the way.

Let's start simple. Suppose that you have a Stage Five (ideology) society and you want to move them just one step to Stage Six (live and let live). You would certainly start with a temporary move using questions and triggers. But then you will have to back it up with helping them to do the work needed to complete Stage Five so that they can move on permanently and not be pulled back.

The work for Stage Five includes moving your ideology from being based on specific beliefs, issues and rules to being based on principles instead. You will then need exercises that show how everyone's principals are largely all the same. See the various tasks listed in Stage Five of the main book, *Purna Asatti*. Take the homework designed for individuals there and apply that to the society at large.

So how do you get an entire society to do the homework? That's the tough part. If you could turn it into a game, that would be ideal. It's a lot easier to work one person at a time and spread virally from there but that takes time.

But suppose a society could benefit from just their leaders shifting stages, as opposed to the entire country shifting?

That would be a great opportunity to apply techniques to shift just those individual leaders into more beneficial stages. Perhaps there would be a ripple effect through the society.

But here's the thing... societies are just a collection of individuals. And individuals are just that... individual. You cannot make them do anything, and you should not want to force anything on anyone. Free will is the most important thing we have as humans on this Earth. You can try to affect someone without their knowledge, asking questions and posing triggers, but they don't have to choose to pay any attention. They do not have to choose to consider it at all.

So keep it ethical out there! See the humanity within your own society, and others. Change yourself, and you change the world. That will always be what it comes down to.

Global Peace In Our Lifetime - Covering Humanity In 32 Steps

Global peace is one of those goals that everyone would like to see happen, but at the same time thinks is impossible. How do you get 8 BILLION people to stop fighting and start helping each other?

An acquaintance in Afghanistan once told me that there is no hope for peace in his country. Generation after generation know only war. How can they even imagine peace, when they have never seen it? While I don't doubt a significant lack of hope in that country, from the outside we all have faith and hope that peace can be restored there one day. But faith and hope are not a strategy. Action is required.

There are amazing people working this from the top. The Peace One Day initiative, founded by Jeremy Gilley, asks world leaders, individuals and even insurgent groups to pause all fighting for one single day of nonviolence every September 21st. And it works. The International Day of Peace has been adopted by an increasing number of heads of state and even terrorist groups. Let me repeat that... terrorist groups agreed to a day of peace and nonviolence. Just let that sink in.

This day allows medical NGOs to go into conflict zones and deliver needed vaccinations and medical care to those who would not normally have access to it. Nobody thought it could be done. But they did it. How? They wrote letters, they travelled the world and they simply asked. So clearly there is more than hope for peace in Afghanistan and the entire world. There is an established day.

This kind of top-down effort has immediate impact, and some significant ripple effects, such as a 70% reduction in violence that lasts for weeks. But how do you turn one day into everyday? That is where the bottom-up approach comes in. You have to solve the source of the problem... the reason there is violence in the first place. How? We will get there...

Now take a moment to think about another deeply related subject... your own personal journey. Your journey of self development, asking the big questions, looking inside yourself to find your truth; your path to personal peace. As you travel this path, you make peace with yourself, with others, and with your world. You accept yourself, you accept others (even if you disagree with them), and you arrive at a beautiful perspective on yourself, others and life. You are personally at peace, even if you live in a stressful environment.

At some point, you decide to live and let live. You stop having grudges, and you stop getting angry and offended, because you can see the humanity in others and in yourself. When you reach this stage (Stage Six and above on the cycle of human development), you do not start conflict, war or violence. You just have no interest in it. Other parts of life are so much more interesting and exciting.

What if every person in a particular town had reached Stage Six (live and let live)? It would be a very peaceful town where people pursue their own paths of interest and help their neighbors when in need. Now, what if everyone in the world had reached Stage Six? It would be a very peaceful world. Entire counties would have no interest in war or violence. This would affect their choice of leaders, their governments at large, and every facet of their lives.

But let's get real. You will never have one hundred percent of humanity in Stage Six. You see, new people are always being born. 250 new lives enter this world every minute. And they must traverse the cycle of human development just like the rest of us. They must start with Stage One and address each stage in turn.

So there will always be people in Stage Three, focused on their own needs; disregarding others and hurting others to fulfill their own ends. And there will always be people in Stage Five, so focused on their ideologies that they cannot see their own humanity much less the humanity of others. In short, there will always be some small segment of humanity who is willing to hurt others and start violence. This is statistically unavoidable.

But what if the overwhelming majority of humanity was past all of that? What if the number of people in Stage Three and Stage Five is so small that their negative effect is functionally neutralized? What if each town and neighborhood connects deeply with each other, offering the kind of real connection that will naturally move these individuals to later stages? What if at any one moment, the number of people traversing these more challenging stages is so small that calls for violence and exploitation never achieve critical mass? That would be a very peaceful world indeed.

So the answer to lasting global peace is to help each individual find personal peace for themselves.

Now, suppose you already found personal peace for yourself. Could you guide someone else, a dear friend or relative, though that journey? Of course you can. Especially if you had a roadmap they could use to largely guide themselves. If you mentor them a little based on your own experience, and you encourage them in their journey, they will achieve that personal peace much faster (months instead of years). Can you help TWO people in this way? Of course! It costs nothing and takes shockingly little of your time.

What if you mentored two people to achieve personal peace. And then they mentored two people each. And they, in turn, mentored two people each. You get the idea. For the math geeks out there, it's a Geometric Series! In the beginning you have affected the lives of two people, then a total of six people, ... but 32 steps after you start, you have affected over 8.5 BILLION people!

And THAT is entirely possible. First help yourself, then help two others and encourage them to help two others. If one individual can reach personal peace in six to twelve months, then we are quite realistically less than 32 years from lasting global peace. And possibly a lot closer than that.

Because most people are in the Stage Four to Stage Six range already, I believe we are more like fifteen years away. And all YOU have to do is spend six to twelve months HELPING YOURSELF, and then six to twelve months helping just TWO other people that you care about. That's it! Sit back and watch your tree branch grow.

———

Support For Your Journey

———

LastingPeace.org

Most people never know how many others they have truly impacted. So I made a website to track the tree as it grows and to act as a global database of critical resources. It is absolutely free to all of humanity.

LastingPeace.org is here to make sure you have the Roadmap and the resources to make your own personal development journey, and that of others, efficient, effective and even fun and to track your tree branch as it grows from your neighborhood across the whole world.

If you feel called to be involved, to take that journey for yourself and/or to mentor even just two others on their own journey of personal discovery, please join us. There are databases of great books and podcasts by stage and task, mentors ready to help, and the complete roadmap from the book *Purna Asatti*.

Starting To Mentor Others

Once you find yourself comfortably in Stage Six (Live And Let Live), it's time to help two others do the same. If you find this intimidating, don't worry! That is pretty common. You see, even though you have been through it yourself, you might think you are not ready to mentor someone else through it. But you are so much more ready than you know!

If you can cook a meal, you can teach someone else how to cook that meal, right? All you are doing is helping someone else do exactly what you have already done. But who? You certainly don't want to force it on anyone who is not interested.

You will find that life has a way of bringing you the two people you need to help. Just be on the lookout for them. They may be your good friends, a family member, or someone you just happen to meet. Who do you know who is going through a rough time? Who do you know who is not enjoying a life of peace and joy? Who comes to you for advice? Here's how you do it...

- Update your profile on LastingPeace.org to show that you are in Stage Six and taking new students.

- Your first two students must be at no charge. After that, you will earn your Mentor title and can charge all you like, IF you care to take on any more.

- Just show others to the website and share your experience.

- Get them started. As soon as they sign up, they will start getting an email course guiding them through exactly what to do.

- Check in with them weekly to answer their questions based on your own experience.

- Meanwhile, continue your own growth!

Remember... you only need to help two others, encourage them to help two others as well, and watch your tree branch grow!

If you just cannot bring yourself to help two others right now, don't judge yourself harshly. You are exactly where you need to be. Just continue your own growth and the time will come.

Here are the most common questions that I get from my students as they start to help others...

But I'm no expert!

And no one expects you to be. You are just human, going through this experience of growth, helping others through nothing more than your own experience. Your own humanity is enough.

How do I bring it up?

Keep it simple. If someone comes to you for advice, just tell them about what worked for you in this process. Tell them you would be happy to guide them through it. Send them the link. Tell them it is not about money, it's about global peace one person at a time and it's WORKING.

What if I'm not good enough to help them?

If you are human, you are good enough. We are here on this Earth to help each other. Go back and do the exercises from Stage Six on breaking the trance of unworthiness. You are so very worthy and you are more ready than you know. Someone needs you and you are equal to the task.

But I still have issues I am working out.

We all do! That work is never done. We are in constant evolution and growth. There is no time like the present!

What if they are just not ready?

This is important... don't force people into this journey if they are not ready. This journey is about helping people who are ready to be helped and want to take this journey for themselves. By NO means should you ever push the subject. If they have seen the site and understand the concept and are not ready, don't bring it up again. Everyone takes this journey in some form in their own time, and in their own way.

Questions, Answers And Additional Resources

Do you have questions about what you have read here? Go to KathrynColleen.com and send in your questions. Kathryn will answer you back as quickly as possible and may include your question on the podcast or blog.

Also at KathrynColleen.com, you will find:

- Links to the full edition of the book, *Purna Asatti*, which includes specific exercises and how-to for each stage and task plus art and poetry for a different perspective on each stage.

- The music album, *Purna Asatti - Music For Complete Connection*, that accompanies the book.

- The podcast, *On Life And Being Human*, where many of your questions may be answered.

- Other useful books, albums, essays and art by Kathryn Colleen.

About The Author

Dr. Amy "Kathryn Colleen" Messegee, PhD RMT is an American-born author, composer and artist better known for her foundational work: *Purna Asatti*, a process and practice that uses connection to self, others and every aspect of your life for managing challenges and accelerating self development.

Her summer job at 16 was doing scientific research at NASA. Before her 25th birthday she earned her PhD in Mathematics and was speaking to conferences on human reasoning and how to make the infinite finite. A hyper-polymath, her career has enjoyed a ride through...

- academia (as a professor of Mathematics),

- defense technology (as a Scientist, CTO, and DARPA Program Manager),

- online media (as founder of a business website and video podcast with a reach of 1.3 million),

- venture capital (advising VC firms on evaluating technologies and reading the founders for their true intent),

- private education (as founder of a local network of elite tutors and private instructors),

- and her current passion: global peace, human connection and energy work.

In each of these, the theme is always the same: aggregating seemingly unrelated perspectives to distill a new approach for accelerated results. She has published many books, hundreds of articles and papers, dozens of unique art pieces and released multiple music albums.

She is known for taking only four students each year but influences and leads thousands around the world in more than 70 countries through speaking, writing, music, art and podcasts.

She is a Reiki Master Practitioner/Teacher and is travel-proficient in nine languages which she is learning simultaneously while living out her dream of traveling the world, speaking at pop up events and aggregating insight on life, the universe and being human.

See KathrynColleen.com for more information, books, articles, music, podcasts, and resources.